# Big, Soft Chewy Cookies

# Big, Soft Chewy Cookies

### JILL VAN CLEAVE

**CB**

CONTEMPORARY
BOOKS

CHICAGO

**Library of Congress Cataloging-in-Publication Data**

Van Cleave, Jill.
    Big, soft, chewy cookies / Jill Van Cleave.
        p.    cm.
    Includes index.
    ISBN 0-8092-3969-8 (pbk.)
    1. Cookies.    I. Title.
TX772.V26    1991
641.8'654—dc20                                    91-19819
                                                      CIP

Published by Contemporary Books, Inc.
180 North Michigan Avenue, Chicago, Illinois 60601
Manufactured in the United States of America
International Standard Book Number: 0-8092-3969-8

*For all women who understand that men love soft cookies*

# Table of Contents

• • • • • • • • • • • •

**INDEX** 112

Special thanks for help and guidance
go to Barry Bluestein, Linda Gray, Georgene
Sainati, my mother, and my husband, Bill,
who ate his way through this book.

# Introduction

What is the best way to satisfy the urge for a tasty treat, a mouth-watering aroma, and a warm fuzzy feeling all at the same time? Why, with a cookie, of course! And, as we all know, the best warm fuzzies come from the best kind of cookie—big, soft, and chewy, with blissful textures, sweet surprises, and full of tender crumbs.

The cookies we remember from childhood, the ones that gave us such pleasure and gratification, were not tiny, thin, bland wafers. They were cookie-jar cookies— big enough to fill two small hands, soft enough to wash down with a glass of milk, and chewy enough to let us savor the intoxicating flavor of each delectable bite. Big, soft cookies are nurturing cookies. They are the ones we wish to treat ourselves, our children, and our children's children to.

This book is divided into chapters by cookie types—drop cookies, shaped cookies, and bar cookies.

Drop cookies are the simplest

to make and require the least amount of time to prepare. With these recipes, all you usually have to do is mix the dough, scoop it up in spoonfuls, drop it onto a cookie sheet, and bake. Sometimes you must scoop and roll the dough before placing it onto the cookie sheet, but that is as complicated as it gets to make them.

Exactly as you would expect, to make shaped cookies you roll and cut the dough into shapes or slices, press it out of a pastry bag, or shape it by using a mold. These cookie doughs often require chilling before you shape and bake them.

Bar cookies are baked in square or rectangular baking pans. Brownies are bar cookies, as are layered cookies with a bottom crust and topping or a filling sandwiched between two crusts. Bar cookies require a little more time to bake than drop cookies, but they take no extra effort.

Within the pages of this book, you'll find recipes for all kinds of drop, shaped, and bar cookies—updated favorites such as Classic Chocolate Chip and Oatmeal Cinnamon cookies, holiday and seasonal treats including Big Soft Ginger cookies and Mincemeat Moons with Rum Frosting, timeless and traditional goodies such as Sour Cream Jumbles and Super Duper Snickerdoodles, and a few rather bold, new delights like my Brown Butter Pecan and Orange Marmalade cookies. I urge you to try all of these recipes. After all, while it *may* be possible to live by chocolate chip cookies alone, why limit yourself to just one soft, chewy taste of heaven?

# Tips for Handling, Baking, and Storing Soft Cookies

As easy as soft cookies are to prepare, it is possible to meet defeat. A dough can be mishandled, or a cookie can bake hard in the oven, if the baker is not aware of these few tips that guarantee success:

• When mixing cookie dough, do not overbeat the dough once the dry ingredients have been added. Mix just until the flour has been incorporated into the dough. Overworking the dough will toughen the cookie.

• If, when you are making shaped cookies, the dough is too soft to handle, chill it (in a tightly sealed container) for at least an hour before forming cookies.

• Make sure that your oven is correctly calibrated. Baking cookies at the wrong temperature

3

is a sure way to either undercook or burn them.

- Use only stainless steel or aluminum cookie sheets to bake cookies. Other types of pans may cause cookies to overheat and possibly burn.

- Do not overbake cookies. Remember that cookies will continue to set as they cool.

- Cookies harden naturally as they sit out over time. If you want your cookies soft, consume them within three days. (Most of these cookies freeze beautifully once baked, and they will be soft and yummy when you bring them back to room temperature.)

- Cookies with a high moisture content, especially cookies made with pureed fruit, should not be stored in airtight containers. The moisture in these cookies will cause them to become unpleasantly gummy. After these cookies have cooled, place them on a plate, and loosely cover the plate with a cloth towel or napkin.

- Some cookies become stale faster than others and will need to be wrapped individually in plastic wrap to prevent hardening. Storage directions are indicated in the recipes. In general, store cookies at room temperature, not in the refrigerator.

• • • • • • • • • • • •

## MORE TIPS FOR THE CURIOUS COOK

Experienced bakers generally have inquisitive minds. Have you ever wondered what ingredients contribute to producing soft cookies? Here are some general tips that can be applied to your cookie-baking repertoire:

- Soft-cookie doughs usually have more moisture than doughs for crisp cookies. If your soft-cookie dough looks dry, add an egg or a small amount of a liquid dairy ingredient such as milk, cream, buttermilk, or sour cream.

- Incorporate pureed fruit into a cookie dough for added moisture and flavor. High-moisture dried fruits, such as figs, dates, and prunes, can soften otherwise dry cookies.

- Cake flour will give a more tender crumb to the baked cookie than all-purpose flour.

- An excess of sugar in the dough often results in crisp—not soft—cookies. If you like your cookies soft but very sweet, you can frost them once they are baked and cooled.

5

# 1
# Drop Cookies

# Applesauce Currant Cookies

The spicy, earthy flavors in this soft, cakelike cookie are universally appealing. Bring these along on picnics, to tailgate parties, or as a box-lunch treat.

*Makes about 16 cookies*

. . . . . . . . . . . . . .

*1 cup dried currants (see Note)*
*2½ cups all-purpose flour*
*1 teaspoon allspice*
*½ teaspoon baking soda*
*½ teaspoon salt*
*½ cup (1 stick) unsalted butter, at room temperature*
*1 cup packed dark brown sugar*
*1 cup natural applesauce (no sugar added)*

**1.** Soak currants in warm water for 15 minutes to soften. Drain and set aside.

**2.** Combine flour, allspice, soda, and salt in a bowl. Mix together and set aside.

**3.** In a mixing bowl, cream butter and sugar until fluffy and smooth. Add applesauce and blend. Stir in flour mixture and currants. Cover bowl with plastic wrap and refrigerate for at least 1 hour.

**4.** Heat oven to 375°F.

**5.** Using either an individual ¼-cup measure or a 2-ounce ice-cream scoop, scoop level measures of dough onto ungreased cookie sheets, spacing the scoopfuls 2 inches apart. Bake until cookies are firm to the touch, about 15 minutes. Using a spatula, transfer cookies to a rack and let cool.

*Store cookies in a loosely covered container at room temperature for up to 3 days. These cookies may also be frozen in a tightly covered container for up to 6 months.*

This dough may be refrigerated for up to 3 days before baking or frozen for up to 3 months. Thaw before baking.

**Note:** You may substitute dried cranberries for the currants, if desired.

9

# Banana Blitz Cookies

Ripe bananas provide rich fruit flavor to this soft, iced cookie.

*Makes about 16 cookies*

• • • • • • • • • • • • • •

¾ *cup (1½ sticks) unsalted butter, at room temperature*
*1 cup packed light brown sugar*
*1 cup mashed ripe banana (about 2 bananas)*
½ *teaspoon banana extract*
*2 cups all-purpose flour*
½ *teaspoon mace*
¼ *teaspoon baking soda*
¼ *teaspoon salt*
*1 cup coarsely chopped toasted pecans*
*White Icing (recipe follows)*

**1.** Heat oven to 375°F.

**2.** In a mixing bowl, cream

together butter and sugar until fluffy and smooth. Add mashed banana and extract and blend.

**3.** In a separate bowl, mix together flour, mace, soda, and salt and add to the creamed mixture. Stir in pecans.

**4.** Using an individual ¼-cup measure, scoop level measures of dough onto ungreased cookie sheets, spacing the scoopfuls 2 inches apart. Bake until cookies are firm to the touch, about 15 minutes.

**5.** Transfer cookies to a rack and let cool. Ice cookies only after they have completely cooled.

*Store cookies in a loosely covered container at room temperature for up to 3 days. These cookies may also be frozen, without icing, in a tightly covered container for up to 6 months.*

This dough may be used immediately or covered with plastic wrap and refrigerated for up to 3 days, or frozen for up to 3 months. Thaw before baking.

WHITE ICING
*1 cup confectioners' sugar*
*4–5 teaspoons milk*

**1.** Using a fork, mix sugar and milk together, adding one teaspoon of milk at a time to produce a smooth, thick icing that falls from the fork in a slow stream.

**2.** Drizzle icing over tops of cooled cookies. Let icing harden before serving.

# Black Walnut Butter Cookies

12

Black walnuts are little treasures in the baking chest of good ingredients. These wonderful gems (and sweet butter) give this extra-large cookie its deep, distinctive taste.

*Makes about 14 cookies*

• • • • • • • • • • • • • • •

1 cup (2 sticks) unsalted butter,
    at room temperature
¾ cup packed light brown sugar
2 large eggs
1 teaspoon vanilla extract
2 cups all-purpose flour
½ teaspoon baking soda
½ teaspoon salt
1 cup chopped black walnuts

1. Heat oven to 350°F.

2. In a mixing bowl, cream butter and sugar together until fluffy and smooth. Add eggs and vanilla and blend.

3. In a separate bowl, mix together flour, baking soda, and salt and add to creamed mixture. Stir in walnuts.

4. Using either an individual ¼-cup measure or a 2-ounce ice-cream scoop, scoop level measures of dough onto ungreased cookie sheets, spacing the scoopfuls 3 inches apart. Bake until cookies are golden brown, about 15 minutes.

5. Using a spatula, transfer cookies to a rack and let cool.

*Store cookies in an airtight jar or tin at room temperature for up to 3 days. These cookies may also be frozen in a tightly covered container for up to 6 months.*

This dough may be used immediately or covered with plastic wrap and refrigerated for up to 5 days, or frozen for up to 3 months. Thaw before baking.

13

# Brown Butter Pecan Cookies

In this tasty cookie the combination of toasted pecans and butter melted until golden brown results in a delectable taste sensation reminiscent of pralines.

*Makes about 12 cookies*

. . . . . . . . . . . . . . .

*1 cup coarsely chopped pecans*
*¾ cup (1½ sticks) unsalted butter*
*1½ cups all-purpose flour*
*½ cup cake flour*
*¼ teaspoon baking soda*
*¼ teaspoon salt*
*2 large eggs*
*1 cup packed light brown sugar*
*½ teaspoon vanilla extract*

**1.** Heat oven to 350°F.

**2.** Spread pecans in a baking dish and toast in oven for 10 minutes. Remove and set aside.

**3.** Melt butter in a skillet over medium-low heat until just browned. (Be careful not to let it burn.) Immediately remove from heat and transfer to a small bowl to stop the cooking. Set aside to cool.

**4.** In a bowl, mix together both flours, soda, and salt. In a separate bowl, beat eggs and sugar until smoothly blended. Add vanilla, then add cooled browned butter and blend. Stir in the flour mixture and toasted pecans.

**5.** Using either an individual ¼-cup measure or a 2-ounce ice-cream scoop, scoop level measures of dough onto greased cookie sheets, spacing the scoopfuls 2½ inches apart.

**6.** Bake until cookies are golden brown and firm to the touch, about 15 minutes. Using a spatula, transfer cookies to a rack and let cool.

*Store cookies in an airtight plastic storage bag, or wrap cookies individually in plastic wrap and store at room temperature for up to 3 days. These cookies may also be frozen in a tightly covered container for up to 6 months.*

This dough may be used immediately or covered with plastic wrap and refrigerated for up to 4 hours before baking.

# Butter-scotch Cookies

A simple-looking cookie that packs a drop-dead rich butterscotch taste. This is definitely a crowd pleaser.

*Makes about 16 cookies*

• • • • • • • • • • • • • •

1 cup (2 sticks) unsalted butter,
    at room temperature
1½ cups packed dark brown
    sugar
1 large egg
3 tablespoons whipping cream
1 teaspoon vanilla extract
2 cups all-purpose flour
1 cup cake flour
1 teaspoon baking soda
½ teaspoon salt

**1.** Heat oven to 375°F.

**2.** In a mixing bowl, cream butter and sugar until smooth. Add the egg, cream, and vanilla and blend. In a separate bowl, mix together both flours, baking soda, and salt and add to creamed mixture.

**3.** Using either an individual ¼-cup measure or a 2-ounce ice-cream scoop, scoop level measures of dough onto ungreased cookie sheets, spacing the scoopfuls 2 inches apart.

**4.** Bake until cookies are golden and firm to the touch, about 15 minutes. Using a spatula, transfer cookies to a rack and let cool.

*To prevent hardening, wrap cookies individually in plastic wrap and store at room temperature for up to 3 days. These cookies may also be frozen in a tightly covered container for up to 6 months.*

This dough may be used immediately or covered with plastic wrap and refrigerated for up to 5 days, or frozen for up to 3 months. Thaw before baking.

17

# Cardamom Buttermilk Cookies

A thin, crisp crust envelops this very tender, cardamom-scented cookie. It's wonderful with a good strong cup of coffee in the morning.

*Makes about 20 cookies*

• • • • • • • • • • • • •

½ cup (1 stick) unsalted butter,
   at room temperature
1 cup packed light brown sugar
1 large egg
½ cup buttermilk
2 cups all-purpose flour
1½ teaspoons cardamom
½ teaspoon baking soda
¼ teaspoon salt

1. Heat oven to 350°F.

2. In a mixing bowl, cream

together butter and sugar until smooth. Add egg and blend. Add buttermilk and blend again.

**3.** In a separate bowl, mix together flour, cardamom, baking soda, and salt and add to creamed mixture.

**4.** Scoop 2 rounded tablespoons of dough and roll together to form each cookie. Drop dough onto ungreased cookie sheets, spacing the cookies 2 inches apart.

**5.** Bake until cookies are golden brown and firm to the touch, about 15 minutes. Using a spatula, transfer cookies to a rack and let cool.

*Store cookies in an airtight plastic storage bag at room temperature for up to 3 days.*

*These cookies may also be frozen in a tightly covered container for up to 6 months.*

This dough may be used immediately or covered with plastic wrap and refrigerated for up to 5 days, or frozen for up to 3 months. Thaw before baking.

# Chocolate Cherry Cookies

Sweet morsels of candied cherry are hidden inside this soft cookie, rich with chocolate and sour cream.

*Makes about 18 cookies*

• • • • • • • • • • • • • •

*2 ounces unsweetened chocolate*
*½ cup (1 stick) unsalted butter, at room temperature*
*1 cup packed dark brown sugar*
*1 large egg*
*1 teaspoon vanilla extract*
*½ cup sour cream*
*1½ cups all-purpose flour*
*½ teaspoon baking soda*
*¼ teaspoon salt*
*¾ cup coarsely chopped glacé red cherries*
*9 whole glacé cherries for garnish*

1. Heat oven to 350°F.

2. Cut chocolate into pieces and place in the top of a double boiler or in a microwavable dish. Melt in double boiler over simmering water or in microwave oven on High power for 1 to 2 minutes until melted. Stir until smooth and set aside.

3. In a mixing bowl, cream together butter and sugar until smooth. Add egg and vanilla and blend. Add sour cream and blend again. Stir in melted chocolate.

4. In a separate bowl, mix together 1 cup of flour, baking soda, and salt. Add to creamed mixture. In a small bowl, toss the remaining ½ cup flour with the chopped cherries. Stir into dough.

5. Scoop 2 rounded tablespoons dough and roll together to form each cookie. Drop onto ungreased cookie sheets, spacing the cookies 2½ inches apart. Cut each whole cherry in half. Center one half onto each cookie.

6. Bake until cookies are just barely firm to the touch, about 15 minutes. Transfer cookies to a rack and let cool.

*Store cookies in an airtight plastic storage bag at room temperature for up to 3 days. These cookies may also be frozen in a tightly covered container for up to 6 months.*

This dough may be used immediately or covered with plastic wrap and refrigerated for up to 5 days, or frozen for up to 3 months. Thaw before baking.

# Chocolate Chocolate Chip Cookies

Rich and seductive, with chocolate melting into even more chocolate, this cookie is impossible for any chocophile to resist.

*Makes about 18 cookies*

. . . . . . . . . . . . . .

*2 ounces unsweetened chocolate*
*½ cup (1 stick) unsalted butter, at room temperature*
*1 cup granulated sugar*
*1 large egg*
*¼ cup milk*
*1 teaspoon vanilla extract*
*2 cups all-purpose flour*
*1 teaspoon baking powder*
*¼ teaspoon salt*
*1 cup semisweet chocolate chips*

**1.** Heat oven to 350°F.

**2.** Cut chocolate into pieces and place in the top of a double boiler or in a microwavable dish. Melt in double boiler over barely simmering water or in microwave oven on High power for 1 to 2 minutes until melted. Stir until smooth and set aside.

**3.** In a mixing bowl, cream together butter and sugar until smooth. Add egg, milk, and vanilla and blend. Add melted chocolate and blend again.

**4.** In a separate bowl, mix together flour, baking powder, and salt and add to creamed mixture. Stir in chocolate chips.

**5.** Scoop dough into 1½-inch balls and arrange on ungreased cookie sheets, spaced 2 inches apart. Bake until firm to the touch, about 15 minutes. Using a spatula, transfer cookies to a rack and let cool.

*Store cookies in an airtight plastic storage bag at room temperature for up to 5 days. These cookies may also be frozen in a tightly covered container for up to 6 months.*

This dough may be used immediately or covered with plastic wrap and refrigerated for up to 5 days, or frozen for up to 3 months. Thaw before baking.

23

# Chocolate Mint Cookies

Candy makers aren't the only ones who can combine chocolate with mint for an unbeatable flavor! Try these for a special taste treat. A creamy icing provides the crowning touch.

*Makes about 18 cookies*

. . . . . . . . . . . . . . .

4 ounces bittersweet or semisweet
   chocolate
½ cup (1 stick) unsalted butter
1 cup packed light brown sugar
1 large egg
¼ cup whipping cream
1 teaspoon peppermint extract
1¾ cups cake flour
½ teaspoon baking powder
¼ teaspoon salt
Mint Cream Icing (see Index)

1. Heat oven to 350°F.

2. Cut chocolate and butter into pieces and combine in the top of a double boiler or in a microwavable dish. Melt in double boiler over barely simmering water or in microwave oven on High power for about 2 minutes, stirring occasionally. Set aside and let cool to room temperature.

3. In a mixing bowl, beat together sugar and egg until blended. Add cream and peppermint extract. Stir in cooled chocolate mixture and blend.

4. In a separate bowl, mix together flour, baking powder, and salt. Add to creamed mixture.

5. Scoop 2 level tablespoons of dough and roll together to form each cookie. Drop onto ungreased cookie sheets, spacing the cookies 2½ inches apart.

6. Bake until tops of cookies look crackled, about 12 minutes. (Cookies will still feel soft.) Transfer cookies to a rack and let cool.

7. When cookies have cooled completely, drizzle tops with Mint Cream Icing.

*Store cookies in an airtight jar or tin at room temperature for up to 3 days. These cookies may also be frozen, without icing, in a tightly covered container for up to 6 months.*

This dough may be used immediately or covered with plastic wrap and refrigerated for up to 5 days, or frozen for up to 3 months. Thaw before baking.

# Chocolate Peanut Butter Cookies

These cookies are sure to become lunch box favorites! Full of great cocoa flavor, plenty of peanut butter, and nuggets of melted chips, these goodies are crispy on the edges and pillow-soft in the center.

*Makes about 11 cookies*

• • • • • • • • • • • • • •

½ cup (1 stick) unsalted butter,
    at room temperature
½ cup chunky peanut butter
1 cup packed dark brown sugar
1 large egg
1 teaspoon vanilla extract
1 cup all-purpose flour
¼ cup unsweetened cocoa
    powder
½ teaspoon baking soda
½ cup semisweet chocolate chips

1. Heat oven to 350°F.

2. In a mixing bowl, cream together butter, peanut butter, and brown sugar until fluffy and smooth. Add egg and vanilla and blend.

3. In a separate bowl, mix together flour, cocoa powder, and baking soda and add to creamed mixture. Stir in chocolate chips.

4. Using either an individual ¼-cup measure or a 2-ounce ice-cream scoop, scoop level measures of dough onto greased cookie sheets, spacing the scoopfuls 2 inches apart.

5. Bake until cookies are firm to the touch, about 18 minutes. After removing cookies from oven, let them set for 2 minutes. Then use a spatula to transfer cookies to a rack and let cool.

*To prevent hardening, wrap each cookie individually in plastic wrap and store at room temperature for up to 3 days. These cookies may also be frozen in a tightly covered container for up to 6 months.*

This dough may be used immediately or covered with plastic wrap and refrigerated for up to 5 days, or frozen for up to 3 months. Thaw before baking.

# Chunky Peanut Butter Cookies

For peanut butter lovers only! Forget the calories and indulge yourself on this one. If you don't have extra-chunky peanut butter on hand, you can use creamy instead and add ½ cup chopped peanuts to the cookie dough.

*Makes about 12 cookies*

• • • • • • • • • • • • •

½ cup (1 stick) unsalted butter,
  at room temperature
⅔ cup extra-chunky peanut
  butter
1 cup packed light brown sugar
2 large eggs
1 cup all-purpose flour
1 cup finely ground
  old-fashioned oats

1. Heat oven to 350°F.

2. In a mixing bowl, cream butter, peanut butter, and sugar until smooth. Add eggs and blend. Stir flour and ground oats into creamed mixture.

3. Using either an individual ¼-cup measure or a 2-ounce ice-cream scoop, scoop level measures of dough onto ungreased cookie sheets, spacing the scoopfuls 2 inches apart. Bake until cookies are golden brown, 18-20 minutes.

4. Using a spatula, transfer cookies to a rack and let cool.

*To prevent hardening, wrap each cookie individually in plastic wrap and store at room temperature for up to 3 days.*

*These cookies may also be frozen in a tightly covered container for up to 6 months.*

This dough may be used immediately or covered with plastic wrap and refrigerated for up to 5 days, or frozen for up to 3 months. Thaw before baking.

29

# Classic Chocolate Chip Cookies

Could there be life without chocolate chip cookies? They are still the single most popular cookie in America. This one truly is classic—no tricks, just a chewy cookie bursting with chocolate flavor.

*Makes about 12 cookies*

• • • • • • • • • • • • • •

*½ cup (1 stick) unsalted butter, at room temperature*
*½ cup packed dark brown sugar*
*½ cup granulated sugar*
*1 large egg*
*2 tablespoons milk*
*1 teaspoon vanilla extract*
*1 cup all-purpose flour*
*½ cup cake flour*
*½ teaspoon baking powder*
*¼ teaspoon salt*
*1 cup semisweet chocolate chips*
*½ cup coarsely chopped walnuts*

1. Heat oven to 375°F.

2. In a mixing bowl, cream together butter and both sugars until smooth. Add the egg, milk, and vanilla and blend.

3. In a separate bowl, mix together both flours, baking powder, and salt and add to the creamed mixture. Stir in the chocolate chips and walnuts.

4. Using either an individual ¼-cup measure or a 2-ounce ice-cream scoop, scoop level measures of dough onto greased cookie sheets, spacing the scoopfuls 2 inches apart. Bake until cookies are browned and firm to the touch, about 15 minutes.

5. Using a spatula, transfer cookies to a rack and let cool.

*To prevent hardening, wrap each cookie individually in plastic wrap and store at room temperature for up to 3 days. These cookies may also be frozen in a tightly covered container for up to 6 months.*

This dough may be used immediately or covered with plastic wrap and refrigerated for up to 5 days, or frozen for up to 3 months. Thaw before baking.

31

# Coco Loco No-Bake Cookies

Almost a candy, these no-bake cookies are quick to make—and quick to be devoured. All you need is a saucepan, a spoon, and a hankering for a taste of chocolate paradise.

*Makes about 18 cookies*

. . . . . . . . . . . . . . .

1 cup granulated sugar
¼ cup (½ stick) unsalted butter
⅓ cup whipping cream
2 tablespoons unsweetened cocoa powder
½ teaspoon vanilla extract
¼ cup creamy peanut butter
1½ cups quick-cooking oats
½ cup raisins

**1.** Line a cookie sheet with waxed paper and set aside.

**2.** In a saucepan, combine sugar, butter, cream, and cocoa powder. Heat and stir until smoothly blended. Bring mixture to a full rolling boil and boil for 1 minute.

**3.** Remove from heat and stir in vanilla and peanut butter until well blended. Add oats and raisins and keep stirring until mixture is thick.

**4.** To form each cookie, scoop 1 heaping tablespoon and drop onto the waxed paper. Set cookies aside to cool and harden.

*Store cookies in an airtight plastic storage bag at room temperature for up to 3 days. Do not freeze.*

# Four-Spice Fantasies

The addition of a surprise ingredient—a hint of pepper—makes these cookies taste fantastic. And while they are baking, lovely, spicy aromas will fill the kitchen.

*Makes about 18 cookies*

• • • • • • • • • • • • •

2½ cups all-purpose flour
¾ teaspoon cinnamon, plus
   ¼ teaspoon for garnish
½ teaspoon allspice
½ teaspoon ground cloves
½ teaspoon white pepper
½ teaspoon baking soda
¼ teaspoon salt
½ cup (1 stick) plus
   3 tablespoons unsalted
   butter, at room temperature
⅔ cup granulated sugar
⅓ cup dark corn syrup
1 large egg

1. Heat oven to 375°F.

2. Combine flour, ¾ teaspoon cinnamon, the remaining spices, baking soda, and salt in a bowl. Mix together and set aside.

3. In a separate bowl, cream butter and sugar until smooth. Add corn syrup and egg and blend. Add the flour mixture and stir to form stiff dough.

4. Roll into 1½-inch balls and drop onto ungreased cookie sheets, spacing the balls 2½ inches apart. Sprinkle tops with the cinnamon reserved for garnish.

5. Bake until just barely firm, about 13 minutes. Do not overbake. Using a spatula, transfer cookies to a rack and let cool.

*To prevent hardening, wrap each cookie individually in plastic wrap and store at room temperature for up to 3 days. These cookies also may be frozen in a tightly covered container for up to 6 months.*

This dough may be used immediately or covered with plastic wrap and refrigerated for up to 5 days, or frozen for up to 3 months. Thaw before baking.

# Fresh Carrot Munchies

These buttery delights guarantee satisfaction for the sweet tooth with a delicate crunch of nourishing carrot in every bite.

*Makes about 12 cookies*

• • • • • • • • • • • • •

¾ cup (1½ sticks) unsalted butter, at room temperature
¾ cup granulated sugar
1 cup shredded raw carrot
½ cup shredded sweetened coconut
Grated rind of 1 lemon (about 1 teaspoon)
2 cups all-purpose flour
1 teaspoon baking powder
½ teaspoon salt

1. Heat oven to 375°F.

2. In a mixing bowl, cream butter and sugar until fluffy and smooth. Add carrot, coconut, and lemon rind and blend.

3. In a separate bowl, mix together flour, baking powder, and salt and add to creamed mixture.

4. Using either an individual ¼-cup measure or a 2-ounce ice-cream scoop, scoop level measures of dough onto ungreased cookie sheets, spacing the scoopfuls 3 inches apart. Bake until cookies are lightly golden and firm to the touch, 15–18 minutes.

5. Using a spatula, transfer cookies to a rack and let cool.

*Store cookies in an airtight jar or tin at room temperature for up to 3 days. These cookies may be frozen in a tightly covered container for up to 6 months.*

This dough may be used immediately or covered with plastic wrap and refrigerated for up to 5 days, or frozen for up to 3 months. Thaw before baking.

37

# Frosted Anise Cookies

This delicious licorice-flavored treat has a slightly domed top—perfect for covering with buttery sweet frosting. The cookie's outer crispness yields to a soft, melt-in-your-mouth interior.

*Makes about 20 cookies*

. . . . . . . . . . . . . . . .

3 large eggs
1 cup granulated sugar
¼ cup (½ stick) unsalted butter, melted
1½ teaspoons anise seed
½ teaspoon anise extract
2 cups all-purpose flour
1 teaspoon baking powder
½ teaspoon salt
Anise Butter Frosting (recipe follows)

1. Heat oven to 375°F.

2. In a mixing bowl, beat together eggs and sugar until smooth. Add melted butter, anise seed, and anise extract and blend.

3. In a separate bowl, mix together flour, baking powder, and salt. Add to the creamed mixture and stir until batter stiffens into a dough.

4. Scoop 2 level tablespoons of dough and roll together to form each cookie. Place onto greased cookie sheets, spacing the cookies 2 inches apart. Bake until cookies are firm to the touch and browned on bottom edges, about 12 minutes.

5. Transfer cookies to a rack and let cool. When cookies are completely cool, frost with Anise Butter Frosting.

*Store cookies in an airtight jar or tin at room temperature for up to 3 days. These cookies may also be frozen, without frosting, in a tightly covered container for up to 6 months.*

This dough may be used immediately or covered with plastic wrap and set aside at room temperature for up to 4 hours. Do not freeze.

## ANISE BUTTER FROSTING

*¼ cup (½ stick) unsalted butter, melted*
*1 teaspoon anise extract*
*1 cup confectioners' sugar*

1. In a bowl, stir together melted butter and anise extract. Gradually add sugar, mixing until frosting is creamy and spreadable.

2. Immediately frost cooled cookies. Let frosting harden before serving cookies.

# Glazed Yogurt-Orange Cookies

40

The word *cookie* comes from the Dutch word *koekje*, which means "little cake." These soft, tender cookies justify the original definition, and the tasty orange glaze accentuates the citrus flavor.

*Makes about 20 cookies*

• • • • • • • • • • • • • • •

1 cup (2 sticks) unsalted butter, at room temperature
1½ cups granulated sugar
1 cup plain lowfat yogurt
Grated peel of 2 oranges (about 2 tablespoons)
1 teaspoon orange extract
3 cups all-purpose flour
1 teaspoon baking soda
½ teaspoon salt
Orange Glaze (recipe follows)

**1.** Heat oven to 375°F.

**2.** In a mixing bowl, cream butter and sugar until smooth. Add yogurt, orange peel, and extract and blend.

**3.** In a separate bowl, mix together flour, baking soda, and salt and add to the creamed mixture.

**4.** Using either an individual ¼-cup measure or a 2-ounce ice-cream scoop, scoop level measures of dough onto ungreased cookie sheets, spacing the scoopfuls 2½ inches apart.

**5.** Bake cookies until they are lightly golden and feel firm to the touch, about 15 minutes. Using a spatula, transfer cookies to a rack and let cool.

**6.** When cookies are completely cool, brush with Orange Glaze.

*Store cookies in a loosely covered container at room temperature for up to 3 days. These cookies may also be frozen, without glaze, in a tightly covered container for up to 6 months.*

This dough may be used immediately or covered with plastic wrap and refrigerated for up to 3 days. Do not freeze.

ORANGE GLAZE
*Juice of 2 freshly squeezed oranges (about ½ cup)*
*¼ cup granulated sugar*
*2 teaspoons cornstarch*

**1.** In a small saucepan, mix juice, sugar, and cornstarch. Over low heat, slowly bring to a boil, stirring, until mixture has thickened.

**2.** Remove from heat and let cool until warm. Brush warm glaze over completely cooled cookies.

# Sour Cream Hermits

Variations of this recipe have been passed around for years. The best of them include sour cream, as this recipe does.

*Makes about 18 cookies*

• • • • • • • • • • • • • • •

½ cup (1 stick) unsalted butter, at room temperature
1 cup packed dark brown sugar
½ cup sour cream
1 large egg
1½ cups all-purpose flour
1 teaspoon cinnamon
½ teaspoon allspice
½ teaspoon baking soda
¼ teaspoon salt
1 cup chopped pitted dates (see Note)
1 cup chopped walnuts (see Note)

1. Heat oven to 350°F.

2. In a mixing bowl, cream butter and brown sugar until creamy smooth. Add sour cream and egg and blend.

3. In a separate bowl, mix together flour, spices, baking soda, and salt and add to the creamed mixture. Stir in dates and walnuts.

4. Scoop 2 rounded tablespoons of dough and roll together to form each cookie. Drop dough onto greased cookie sheets, spacing the cookies 2½ inches apart.

5. Bake until cookies are firm to the touch, about 15 minutes. Using a spatula, transfer cookies to a rack and let cool.

*Store cookies in an airtight jar or tin at room temperature for up to 3 days. These cookies may also be frozen in a tightly covered container for up to 6 months.*

This dough may be used immediately or covered with plastic wrap and refrigerated for up to 5 days, or frozen for up to 3 months. Thaw before baking.

**Note:** You may substitute raisins and pecans for the dates and walnuts, if desired.

# Light and Dark Chocolate Chunk Cookies

44

Sweet and creamy white chocolate blissfully mingles with bitter dark chocolate in this cookie. The big chunks provide maximum chocolate pleasure.

*Makes about 18 cookies*

• • • • • • • • • • • • • •

¾ cup (1½ sticks) unsalted butter, at room temperature
¾ cup packed light brown sugar
2 large eggs
½ teaspoon almond extract
2¼ cups all-purpose flour
1 teaspoon baking soda
½ teaspoon salt
1 cup sweetened shredded coconut
6 ounces white chocolate, cut into ½-inch chunks
6 ounces bittersweet chocolate, cut into ½-inch chunks

1. Heat oven to 350°F.

2. In a mixing bowl, cream butter and sugar until smooth. Add eggs and almond extract and blend.

3. In a separate bowl, mix together flour, baking soda, and salt and add to the creamed mixture. Stir in coconut and both kinds of chocolate chunks.

4. Using either an individual ¼-cup measure or a 2-ounce ice-cream scoop, scoop level measures of dough onto ungreased cookie sheets, spacing the scoopfuls 2 inches apart.

5. Bake until cookies are lightly golden brown, about 15 minutes. Using a spatula, transfer cookies to a rack and let cool.

*To prevent hardening, wrap each cookie individually in plastic wrap and store at room temperature for up to 3 days. These cookies may also be frozen in a tightly covered container for up to 6 months.*

This dough may be used immediately or covered with plastic wrap and refrigerated for up to 5 days, or frozen for up to 3 months. Thaw before baking.

# Macadamia Nut Macaroons

Nutty and oh, so sweet, this delicate, chewy confection is the perfect companion to vanilla bean ice cream.

*Makes about 16 cookies*

• • • • • • • • • • • •

1 3½-ounce jar macadamia nuts
½ cup granulated sugar
2 large egg whites
⅔ cup confectioners' sugar
½ cup cake flour

**1.** Heat oven to 325°F.

**2.** In a food processor or food grinder, grind the nuts finely with the granulated sugar. Set aside.

**3.** Using an electric mixer, beat egg whites in a bowl until thickened. Add confectioners' sugar and beat until shiny. Stir in the nut mixture and flour. Set dough aside for 15 minutes until firm.

**4.** To form each cookie, scoop 1 rounded tablespoon of dough and drop onto a greased and floured cookie sheet. Space the scoopfuls 3 inches apart.

**5.** Bake until cookies are lightly golden, about 12 minutes. Remove cookies from oven and let them set for 2 minutes. Then use a spatula to carefully transfer cookies to a rack and let cool.

*Store cookies in an airtight plastic storage bag at room temperature for up to 5 days. Do not freeze.*

47

# Mincemeat Moons with Rum Frosting

These tender and flavorful cookies will be a welcome change from mincemeat pie at holiday time. The frosting adds a festive touch—just like wrapping on a gift!

*Makes about 13 cookies*

• • • • • • • • • • • • • •

½ cup (1 stick) unsalted butter, at room temperature
¾ cup granulated sugar
2 large eggs
1 cup prepared mincemeat
2 cups all-purpose flour
1 teaspoon baking powder
½ teaspoon salt
*Rum Frosting (recipe follows)*

**1.** Heat oven to 375°F.

**2.** In a mixing bowl, cream butter and sugar until smooth.

Add eggs and blend. Stir in mincemeat.

**3.** In a separate bowl, mix together flour, baking powder, and salt and add to creamed mixture.

**4.** Using either an individual ¼-cup measure or a 2-ounce ice-cream scoop, scoop level measures of dough onto lightly greased cookie sheets, spacing the scoopfuls 2 inches apart. Flatten each cookie slightly. Bake until cookies are lightly golden and firm to the touch, 15–17 minutes.

**5.** Using a spatula, transfer cookies to a rack and let cool. After cookies have completely cooled, frost with Rum Frosting.

*Store cookies in a loosely covered container at room temperature for up to 3 days.*

*These cookies may also be frozen, without frosting, in a tightly covered container for up to 6 months.*

This dough may be used immediately or covered with plastic wrap and refrigerated for up to 5 days, or frozen for up to 3 months. Thaw before baking.

RUM FROSTING
*¼ cup (½ stick) unsalted butter, at room temperature*
*1 cup confectioners' sugar*
*1 tablespoon rum, light or dark*

**1.** In a small bowl, cream butter and sugar until blended. Add rum and stir until frosting is soft and creamy.

**2.** Immediately frost cooled cookies.

# Oatmeal Cinnamon Cookies

Those who like cinnamon sprinkled on their oatmeal in the morning will love these cookies. In fact, try one for a breakfast treat when you need to grab and go.

*Makes about 14 cookies*

• • • • • • • • • • • • • •

2 cups old-fashioned oats
1½ cups all-purpose flour
1½ teaspoons cinnamon
½ teaspoon baking soda
½ teaspoon salt
1 large egg
1 cup granulated sugar
1 cup (2 sticks) unsalted butter,
  melted and cooled
1 tablespoon dark molasses
¼ cup milk
½ cup chopped pecans

1. Heat oven to 350°F.

2. Combine oats, flour, cinnamon, baking soda, and salt in a bowl. Mix together and set aside.

3. In a separate bowl, beat together egg and sugar. Add butter and continue beating. When completely blended, add molasses and milk and blend again. Stir in the oat mixture and the pecans.

4. Using either an individual ¼-cup measure or a 2-ounce ice-cream scoop, scoop level measures of dough onto ungreased cookie sheets, spacing the scoopfuls 2½ inches apart. Bake until cookies are golden brown, about 15 minutes. (Do not overbake.)

5. After removing cookies from oven, let them set for 1 minute.

Then use a spatula to transfer cookies to a rack and let cool.

*To prevent hardening, wrap each cookie individually in plastic wrap and store at room temperature for up to 3 days. These cookies may also be frozen in a tightly covered container for up to 6 months.*

This dough may be used immediately or covered with plastic wrap and refrigerated for up to 5 days, or frozen for up to 3 months. Thaw before baking.

# Oatmeal Coconut White Chocolate Cookies

52

Sweet, crunchy coconut combined with seductive, rich white chocolate guarantees this oatmeal cookie's success.

*Makes about 18 cookies*

• • • • • • • • • • • • •

*1 cup (2 sticks) unsalted butter,
   at room temperature
1 cup packed dark brown sugar
1 large egg
¼ cup milk
1 teaspoon almond extract
2 cups all-purpose flour
2 cups old-fashioned oats
1 teaspoon baking soda
½ teaspoon salt
1 cup sweetened shredded
   coconut
6 ounces white chocolate, cut
   into ½-inch chunks*

1. Heat oven to 350°F.

2. In a mixing bowl, cream butter and sugar until fluffy and smooth. Add egg, milk, and almond extract and blend.

3. In a separate bowl, mix together flour, oats, baking soda, and salt and add to the creamed mixture. Stir in coconut and white chocolate.

4. Using either an individual ¼-cup measure or a 2-ounce ice-cream scoop, scoop level measures of dough onto ungreased cookie sheets, spacing the scoopfuls 2 inches apart.

5. Bake until cookies are golden brown, about 15 minutes. Using a spatula, transfer cookies to a rack and let cool.

*To prevent hardening, wrap each cookie individually in plastic wrap and store at room temperature for up to 3 days. These cookies may also be frozen in a tightly covered container for up to 6 months.*

This dough may be used immediately or covered with plastic wrap and refrigerated for up to 5 days, or frozen for up to 3 months. Thaw before baking.

53

# Oatmeal Walnut Raisin Cookies

54

Turn back the clock to the childhood pleasure and comfort of a cozy kitchen snack with this big, tasty treat.

*Makes about 14 cookies*

• • • • • • • • • • • • •

1½ cups old-fashioned oats
1 cup all-purpose flour
½ teaspoon baking soda
½ teaspoon baking powder
½ teaspoon salt
½ cup (1 stick) plus
   3 tablespoons unsalted
   butter, at room temperature
½ cup packed dark brown sugar
½ cup granulated sugar
1 large egg
1 tablespoon milk
1 teaspoon vanilla extract
1 cup coarsely chopped walnuts
1 cup raisins

1. Heat oven to 350°F.

2. Combine oats, flour, baking soda, baking powder, and salt in a bowl. Mix together and set aside.

3. In a separate bowl, cream butter with both sugars until fluffy and smooth. Add egg, milk, and vanilla and blend until smooth. Stir in the oat mixture, walnuts, and raisins.

4. Using either an individual ¼-cup measure or a 2-ounce ice-cream scoop, scoop level measures of dough onto ungreased cookie sheets, spacing the scoopfuls 3 inches apart. Bake until edges of cookies are golden brown, about 15 minutes. (Do not overbake.)

5. After removing cookies from oven, let them set for 1 minute. Then use a spatula to transfer cookies to a rack and let cool.

*To prevent hardening, wrap each cookie individually in plastic wrap and store at room temperature for up to 3 days. These cookies may also be frozen in a tightly covered container for up to 6 months.*

This dough may be used immediately or covered with plastic wrap and refrigerated for up to 5 days, or frozen for up to 3 months. Thaw before baking.

55

# Old-Fashioned Cream Cookies

In the days when homemakers churned cream into butter, cookies such as these served as inspiration for the laborious task. Use colored candy sprinkles to dress them up, or enjoy them unadorned and fresh from the oven.

*Makes about 18 cookies*

• • • • • • • • • • • • • • • • • •

$1\frac{1}{2}$ *cups all-purpose flour*
$\frac{1}{2}$ *cup cake flour*
$\frac{1}{2}$ *teaspoon baking soda*
$\frac{1}{4}$ *teaspoon salt*
$\frac{1}{4}$ *teaspoon mace*
*2 large eggs*
*1 cup granulated sugar*
$\frac{1}{2}$ *cup whipping cream*
$\frac{1}{3}$ *cup ($5\frac{1}{3}$ tablespoons) unsalted butter, melted and cooled*
$\frac{1}{2}$ *teaspoon vanilla extract*
*Colored sprinkles*

1. Heat oven to 350°F.

2. Combine both flours, baking soda, salt, and mace in a bowl. Mix together and set aside.

3. In a separate bowl, beat together eggs and sugar until smooth. Add cream, butter, and vanilla and blend. Stir in the flour mixture.

4. Scoop 2 rounded tablespoons of dough and roll together to form each cookie. Drop dough onto greased cookie sheets, spacing the cookies 2 inches apart. Decorate tops with colored sprinkles.

5. Bake until cookies are lightly golden and firm to the touch, about 12 minutes. Using a spatula, transfer cookies to a rack and let cool.

*Store cookies in an airtight jar or tin at room temperature for up to 3 days. These cookies may also be frozen in a tightly covered container for up to 6 months.*

This dough may be used immediately or covered with plastic wrap and refrigerated for up to 5 days, or frozen for up to 3 months. Thaw before baking.

57

# Poppy Seed Honey Cookies

Laced with sweet, syrupy honey, these cookies are the perfect down-home treat to serve when family or friends come to visit.

*Makes about 25 cookies*

. . . . . . . . . . . . . .

1 cup honey
½ cup (1 stick) unsalted butter
1 teaspoon baking soda
2 large eggs
2½ cups all-purpose flour
½ teaspoon salt
1½ tablespoons poppy seeds

**1.** In a medium saucepan, combine honey and butter. Bring to a full rolling boil and cook for 1 minute. Remove from heat and stir in baking soda. (Mixture will foam and increase sizably in volume.) Set aside to cool until barely warm.

**2.** Heat oven to 350°F.

**3.** Beat eggs into honey mixture; then stir in flour, salt, and poppy seeds. Stir until dough is very stiff.

**4.** For each cookie, scoop 1 heaping tablespoon of dough and drop onto greased cookie sheets, spacing cookies 2½ inches apart.

**5.** Bake until cookies are firm to the touch, about 10 minutes. (Do not overbake.) Using a spatula, transfer cookies to a rack and let cool.

*Store cookies in an airtight jar or tin at room temperature for up to 5 days. Do not freeze.*

# Prune 'n' Plenty Cookies

A moist, tasty anytime snack packed with a one-two punch of fruit and nuts, these cookies are almost too good to be true.

*Makes about 16 cookies*

• • • • • • • • • • • • • • • •

*2 cups all-purpose flour*
*1 teaspoon cinnamon*
*½ teaspoon baking soda*
*¼ teaspoon ground cloves*
*¼ teaspoon salt*
*½ cup (1 stick) unsalted butter,*
*    at room temperature*
*1 cup packed light brown sugar*
*1 large egg*
*¼ cup orange juice*
*1 cup chopped pitted prunes*
*1 cup chopped walnuts*
*½ cup chopped dried apricots*
*½ cup raisins*

1. Heat oven to 350°F.

2. Combine flour, cinnamon, baking soda, cloves, and salt in a bowl. Mix together and set aside.

3. In a mixing bowl, cream butter and sugar until fluffy and smooth. Add egg and orange juice and blend. Stir in flour mixture, prunes, walnuts, apricots, and raisins.

4. Using either an individual ¼-cup measure or a 2-ounce ice-cream scoop, scoop level measures of dough onto ungreased cookie sheets, spacing the scoopfuls 2½ inches apart. Flatten each to a thickness of ½ inch.

5. Bake until cookies are golden brown, about 15 minutes. Using a spatula, transfer cookies to a rack and let cool.

*Store cookies in an airtight plastic storage bag at room temperature for up to 3 days. These cookies may also be frozen in a tightly covered container for up to 6 months.*

This dough may be used immediately or covered with plastic wrap and refrigerated for up to 5 days, or frozen for up to 3 months. Thaw before baking.

61

# Tart Cherry Raisin Cookies

There is plenty of texture and sweetness in these cookies. They are a good accompaniment to baked apples or poached pears.

*Makes about 12 cookies*

. . . . . . . . . . . . . . .

½ cup (1 stick) unsalted butter, at room temperature
¾ cup granulated sugar
½ cup sour cream
½ teaspoon almond extract
1½ cups all-purpose flour
½ teaspoon baking soda
¼ teaspoon salt
¾ cup raisins
¾ cup dried tart cherries (see Note)

**1.** Heat oven to 375°F.

**2.** In a mixing bowl, cream butter and sugar until smooth.

Add sour cream and almond extract and blend.

**3.** In a separate bowl, mix together flour, baking soda, and salt and add to the creamed mixture. Stir in raisins and cherries.

**4.** Using either an individual ¼-cup measure or a 2-ounce ice-cream scoop, scoop level measures of dough onto ungreased cookie sheets, spacing the scoopfuls 2 inches apart.

**5.** Bake until cookies are lightly golden brown, 15-17 minutes. Using a spatula, transfer cookies to a rack and let cool.

*Store cookies in an airtight jar or tin at room temperature for up to 3 days. These cookies may also be frozen in a tightly covered container for up to 6 months.*

This dough may be used immediately or covered with plastic wrap and refrigerated for up to 5 days, or frozen for up to 3 months. Thaw before baking.

**Note:** You may substitute dried cranberries for the cherries, if desired.

63

# Super Duper Snicker-doodles

64

The distinctive signature of Snickerdoodles is that they are always rolled or dredged in cinnamon sugar before baking. Instead of baking powder, this recipe uses the old-fashioned combination of cream of tartar and baking soda, typical of older-style cake and cookie recipes. This is my rendition of a midwestern Amish recipe my mother found.

*Makes about 14 cookies*

• • • • • • • • • • • • • •

½ cup (1 stick) unsalted butter, at room temperature
¾ cup granulated sugar
1 large egg
1 tablespoon milk
½ teaspoon vanilla extract
1½ cups all-purpose flour
½ teaspoon cream of tartar
¼ teaspoon baking soda
¼ teaspoon salt
2 tablespoons granulated sugar
1 tablespoon cinnamon

**1.** In a mixing bowl, cream together butter and ¾ cup granulated sugar until smooth. Add egg, milk, and vanilla and blend.

**2.** In a separate bowl, mix together flour, cream of tartar, baking soda, and salt and add to the creamed mixture. Cover bowl with plastic wrap and refrigerate for at least 1 hour until dough is firm enough to handle.

**3.** Heat oven to 375°F.

**4.** On a plate, mix 2 tablespoons of sugar with cinnamon. Scoop and roll the dough into 1½-inch balls; then roll in cinnamon sugar to coat all sides. Arrange sugar-coated balls on ungreased cookie sheets, spacing them 2½ inches apart.

**5.** Bake until edges of cookies are firm to the touch, about 12 minutes. (Do not overbake.) Using a spatula, transfer cookies to a rack and let cool.

*Store cookies in an airtight plastic storage bag at room temperature for up to 3 days. These cookies may also be frozen in a tightly covered container for up to 6 months.*

This dough may be covered with plastic wrap and refrigerated for up to 5 days, or frozen for up to 3 months. Thaw before baking.

# Big Soft Almond Cookies

A wonderful almond flavor permeates this soft cookie, leaving a delicate aftertaste that lingers in the memory.

*Makes about 28 cookies*

• • • • • • • • • • • • • •

1 cup (2 sticks) unsalted butter,
  at room temperature
1 cup granulated sugar
2 large eggs
1 cup canned almond filling (see
  Note)
¼ cup milk
3 cups all-purpose flour
½ teaspoon baking soda
¼ teaspoon salt
¼ cup sliced blanched almonds

1. Heat oven to 350°F.

2. In a mixing bowl, cream together butter and sugar until smooth. Add eggs and blend. Add almond filling and milk and blend again.

3. In a separate bowl, mix together flour, baking soda, and salt and add to the creamed mixture.

4. Scoop 2 rounded tablespoons of dough and roll together to form each cookie. Drop dough onto lightly greased cookie sheets, spacing the cookies 2 inches apart. Press sliced almonds onto tops.

5. Bake until cookies are lightly golden and firm to the touch, about 15 minutes. Using a spatula, transfer cookies to a rack and let cool.

*Store cookies in an airtight jar or tin at room temperature for up to 3 days. These cookies may also be frozen in a tightly covered container for up to 6 months.*

This dough may be used immediately or covered with plastic wrap and refrigerated for up to 5 days. Do not freeze.

**Note:** Almond filling is available in ready-to-use 12-ounce cans in most supermarkets.

# Big Soft Ginger Cookies

A delightful combination of spices and the gentle flavor of molasses make these cookies distinctively delicious. They are sure to become real favorites at holiday time.

*Makes about 17 cookies*

• • • • • • • • • • • • •

1½ cups all-purpose flour
¾ cup cake flour
1 teaspoon baking soda
½ teaspoon salt
1 teaspoon ginger
½ teaspoon cinnamon
½ teaspoon ground cloves
¾ cup (1½ sticks) unsalted butter,
    at room temperature
¾ cup packed dark brown sugar
¼ cup dark molasses
2 tablespoons milk
1 large egg
¼ cup granulated sugar

**1.** Combine both flours, baking soda, salt, and spices in a bowl. Mix together and set aside.

**2.** In a separate bowl, cream together butter and brown sugar until fluffy and smooth. Add molasses, milk, and egg and blend. Add flour mixture and blend. Cover dough with plastic wrap and refrigerate for at least 1 hour.

**3.** Heat oven to 375°F.

**4.** To form each cookie, roll 3 tablespoons of chilled dough into a ball. Pour the granulated sugar onto a plate. Roll each dough ball into the sugar to coat all sides. Place dough balls on ungreased cookie sheets and flatten into 3-inch rounds, spacing them 2 inches apart.

**5.** Bake until cookies are firm to the touch and tops are slightly cracked, about 10 minutes. (Do not overbake.) After removing cookies from oven, let them set for 2 minutes. Then use a spatula to transfer cookies to a rack and let cool.

*Store cookies in an airtight plastic storage bag at room temperature for up to 3 days. These cookies may also be frozen in a tightly covered container for up to 6 months.*

This dough may be coverd with plastic wrap and refrigerated for up to 5 days, or frozen for up to 3 months. Thaw before baking.

# Sweet Chocolate Chestnut Smoothies

Nothing is better to shake off a winter chill than a plateful of these soft, smooth-as-silk cookies and mugs of steaming hot cocoa.

*Makes about 20 cookies*

. . . . . . . . . . . . . .

*1 cup (2 sticks) unsalted butter, at room temperature*
*1 cup unsweetened chestnut puree (see Note)*
*2 cups granulated sugar*
*2 large eggs*
*2 teaspoons vanilla extract*
*2 cups all-purpose flour*
*1 teaspoon baking powder*
*1 teaspoon baking soda*
*½ teaspoon salt*
*8 ounces semisweet chocolate or chocolate chips*

**1.** Heat oven to 375°F.

**2.** In a mixing bowl, cream butter, chestnut puree, and sugar until smoothly blended. Add eggs and vanilla and mix until blended.

**3.** In a separate bowl, mix together flour, baking powder, baking soda, and salt and add to the creamed mixture.

**4.** Using either an individual ¼-cup measure or a 2-ounce ice-cream scoop, scoop level measures of dough onto greased cookie sheets, spacing the scoopfuls 2½ inches apart.

**5.** Bake until edges of cookies have browned, about 15 minutes. Using a spatula, transfer cookies to a rack and let cool.

**6.** While cookies are cooling, finely chop the chocolate, place into a small zipper-top plastic storage bag, and seal top. Set bag into a bowl of hot tap water, with sealed top hanging over bowl edge out of water. When chocolate has completely melted, remove bag from water.

**7.** Snip a small hole in one corner of the bag. Squeeze out chocolate, drizzling it decoratively over cooled cookies.

*Store cookies in a loosely covered container at room temperature for up to 3 days. These cookies may also be frozen in a tightly covered container for up to 6 months.*

This dough may be used immediately or covered with plastic wrap and refrigerated for up to 5 days. Do not freeze.

**Note:** Unsweetened chestnut puree is available in the specialty-food sections of most supermarkets.

# 2
# Shaped Cookies

# Apricot Pillows

Buttermilk is the secret ingredient that gives this treat its special taste and tender crumb. A double-layered cookie surrounds a central dollop of fruit filling. Delicious!

*Makes about 20 cookies*

. . . . . . . . . . . .

*½ cup (1 stick) unsalted butter, at room temperature*
*1 cup granulated sugar*
*1 large egg*
*1 teaspoon vanilla extract*
*3 cups all-purpose flour*
*1 teaspoon baking powder*
*½ teaspoon baking soda*
*¼ teaspoon salt*
*½ cup buttermilk*
*1 12-ounce can apricot filling*

1. Heat oven to 375°F.

2. In a mixing bowl, cream butter and sugar until fluffy and smooth. Add egg and vanilla and blend.

3. In a separate bowl, mix together flour, baking powder, baking soda, and salt. Add the flour mixture to the creamed mixture, alternating with buttermilk to form dough.

4. Turn out half the dough onto a lightly floured surface and roll into a 12-inch round. Using a 3-inch round cookie cutter, cut an even number of rounds. Using a 1-inch round cutter, punch out the centers of *half* of the rounds.

5. Arrange the uncut rounds on ungreased cookie sheets. Moisten the outer edges of these with a bit of water, then layer the cut-out rounds on top. Center a rounded teaspoon of apricot filling in the middle hole of each.

6. Bake until cookies are lightly golden around bottom edges and firm to the touch, about 10 minutes. Using a spatula, transfer cookies to a rack and let cool.

7. Repeat with remaining dough, rerolling any dough scraps.

75

*Store cookies in an airtight jar or tin at room temperature for up to 5 days. These cookies may be frozen in a tightly covered container for up to 6 months.*

This dough may be used immediately or covered with plastic wrap and refrigerated for up to 3 days, or frozen for up to 3 months. Thaw before using.

# Big Jelly Buttons

These individual cookie tarts have a buttery, not overly sweet base and can be filled with your choice of fruit preserves or jellies.

*Makes about 14 cookie tarts*

• • • • • • • • • • • • •

1 cup (2 sticks) unsalted butter, at room temperature
½ cup granulated sugar
1 large egg
1½ teaspoons vanilla extract
1½ cups all-purpose flour
1 cup cake flour
1 cup fruit preserves or jelly

1. Heat oven to 350°F.

2. In a mixing bowl, cream butter and sugar until fluffy and smooth. Add egg and vanilla and blend. Add both flours and stir to form a stiff dough.

3. Pat dough into a ball, then roll out on a lightly floured surface to ¼-inch thickness. Using a 3-inch round cookie cutter, cut rounds of dough. Arrange the rounds on ungreased cookie sheets, spacing them 2 inches apart. Using your fingers, raise the outside edges of each dough round to shape into a tart shell. Fill each center depression with 1 level tablespoon of fruit preserves or jelly.

4. Bake until crust is firm but not browned, about 15 minutes. (Jelly will be soft while hot, but will set firm when cool.) Using a spatula, transfer cookies to a rack and let cool.

5. Reroll remaining dough scraps, and repeat cutting, filling, and baking.

*Store cookies in an airtight jar or tin at room temperature for up to 5 days. These cookies may also be frozen in a tightly covered container for up to 6 months.*

This dough may be used immediately or covered with plastic wrap and refrigerated for up to 5 days, or frozen for up to 3 months. Thaw before using.

# Fruit and Cream Cheese Kolackys

78

Kolacky, a pastry beloved in Eastern Europe, has a rich, tender crust of cream cheese that surrounds a sweet, jamlike fruit filling. It is the perfect dessert cookie.

*Makes about 25 cookies*

• • • • • • • • • • • • • •

*½ cup (1 stick) unsalted butter, at room temperature*
*4 ounces cream cheese, at room temperature*
*½ cup granulated sugar*
*1½ cups cake flour*
*1 cup canned fruit filling (prune, cherry, apricot, or blueberry— see Note)*

1. In a mixing bowl, cream butter and cream cheese until blended. Add sugar and beat until smooth. Add flour, ½ cup at a time, and mix into a dough. Press dough into a ball, cover with plastic wrap, and refrigerate at least 1 hour.

2. Heat oven to 350°F.

3. Turn out chilled dough onto a lightly floured surface and roll into a 15-inch circle. Using a 3-inch round cookie cutter, cut rounds of dough.

4. Center 1 rounded teaspoon fruit filling onto each dough round. Form open-topped dumplings by lifting up the outside edges of dough to surround, but not cover, the filling. Arrange cookies on ungreased cookie sheets, spacing them 1½ inches apart.

5. Bake until edges of cookies are golden, about 15 minutes. After removing cookies from oven, let them set for 1 minute. Then use a spatula to transfer cookies to a rack and let cool.

6. Repeat with remaining dough, rerolling any dough scraps.

*Store cookies in an airtight jar or tin at room temperature for up to 3 days. These cookies may also be frozen in a tightly covered container for up to 6 months.*

This dough may be stored in the refrigerator for up to 5 days, or frozen for up to 3 months. Thaw before using.

**Note:** Fruit fillings are available in ready-to-use 12-ounce cans in most supermarkets.

# Creamed Short-bread Cookies

One taste of these tender cookies and you'll find it difficult to stop. Since they are not very sweet, try pairing them with fruit sorbet for a delicious dessert or snack.

*Makes about 12 cookies*

• • • • • • • • • • • • •

½ cup (1 stick) unsalted butter,
   at room temperature
¼ cup confectioners' sugar
¼ cup sour cream
1¼ cups cake flour
¼ teaspoon baking soda
¼ teaspoon salt

1. Heat oven to 350°F.

2. In a mixing bowl, cream butter and sugar until smooth. Add sour cream and blend.

3. In a separate bowl, mix together flour, baking soda, and salt and add to creamed mixture.

4. Turn out dough onto a lightly floured surface and roll to ¼-inch thickness. Using a 2½-inch round cookie cutter, cut rounds of dough. Reroll scraps and cut to use all the dough.

5. Arrange cookies on ungreased cookie sheets, spacing them 1 inch apart. Prick cookie tops with a fork in several places.

6. Bake until cookies are lightly golden, about 15 minutes. (Do not overbake.) Using a spatula, transfer cookies to a rack and let cool.

*Store cookies in an airtight jar or tin at room temperature for up to 3 days. These cookies may be frozen in a tightly covered container for up to 6 months.*

This dough may be used immediately or covered with plastic wrap and refrigerated for up to 3 days, or frozen for up to 3 months. Thaw before using.

# Date Nut Sweeties

82

These addicting cookies deliver triple pleasure with the tantalizing tastes of dates, tangy citrus, and bits of pecan.

*Makes about 14 cookies*

• • • • • • • • • • • • • • •

½ cup (1 stick) unsalted butter, at room temperature
¾ cup granulated sugar
¼ cup sour cream
1½ cups all-purpose flour
½ teaspoon baking soda
½ teaspoon salt
1 8-ounce package pitted dates
Grated rind of 1 orange (about 1 tablespoon)
½ cup chopped pecans

**1.** Cream butter and ½ cup of the sugar until smooth. Add sour cream and blend.

**2.** In a separate bowl, mix together flour, baking soda, and salt and add to creamed mixture. Cover with plastic wrap and refrigerate for at least 1 hour.

**3.** Chop dates with the remaining ¼ cup sugar and the orange rind by hand or in a food processor. Add pecans and continue to chop until mixture has a uniform consistency. Set aside.

**4.** Heat oven to 375°F.

**5.** Turn out chilled dough onto a floured surface and roll into a 14″ × 10″ rectangle. Distribute date filling evenly over dough.

**6.** Beginning with the long side, roll up dough tightly, jelly roll style. Cut crosswise into 1-inch-thick slices.

**7.** Arrange each slice cut side up, and flatten with a spatula to ½-inch thickness. With the spatula, transfer dough slices to ungreased cookie sheets, spacing slices 2 inches apart.

**8.** Bake until edges of cookies are lightly golden and tops are firm, 10–12 minutes. After removing cookies from oven, let them set for 1 minute. Transfer cookies to a rack to cool.

*Store cookies in an airtight jar or tin at room temperature for up to 3 days. These cookies may also be frozen in a tightly covered container for up to 6 months.*

This dough may be stored in the refrigerator for up to 3 days, or frozen for up to 3 months. Thaw before using.

# French Madeleines

These are lovely tea cakes, light as air and soft as a cloud. Traditionally, madeleines are baked in special shell-shaped molds. You can, however, successfully bake these in a mini-muffin tin instead, using the same amount of batter per cookie as with a madeleine pan.

*Makes about 36 cookies*

• • • • • • • • • • •

*1 cup cake flour*
*½ teaspoon baking powder*
*¼ teaspoon salt*
*3 large eggs*
*⅔ cup granulated sugar*
*2 teaspoons grated lemon rind*
*1 teaspoon orange extract (see Note)*
*¾ cup (1½ sticks) unsalted butter, melted and cooled*
*¼ cup confectioners' sugar*

1. Heat oven to 350°F.

2. Sift cake flour, baking powder, and salt into a bowl and set aside.

3. In a separate bowl, use an electric mixer to beat eggs until light in color. Add granulated sugar, lemon rind, and orange extract. Beat on high speed for 2 minutes, until mixture has thickened and volume has slightly increased.

4. Using a rubber spatula, gently stir in the flour mixture, followed by the butter, until completely incorporated. (Batter will be light and spongy.) Spoon 1 rounded tablespoon of batter into each greased madeleine mold or mini-muffin cup.

5. Bake until cookies are lightly golden and firm to the touch, 10-12 minutes. Immediately invert pan over a cooling rack to unmold cookies.

6. While cookies are warm, sift confectioners' sugar over tops. These are particularly good if eaten while still slightly warm.

*Store cookies in an airtight plastic storage bag at room temperature for 3 days or in freezer for up to 6 months. If freezing cookies, omit the dusting of confectioners' sugar.*

**Note:** You may substitute vanilla for the orange extract, if desired.

# Luscious Ladyfingers

These light, spongy cookies are often used to line a mold or provide a base for desserts such as Bavarian cream, chocolate mousse, fruit pudding, or English trifle. They happen to be pretty tasty on their own, as well.

*Makes about 18 cookies*

• • • • • • • • • • • •

3 large eggs, separated
½ cup granulated sugar
½ teaspoon dried orange peel
¼ teaspoon cream of tartar
⅔ cup cake flour
¼ cup confectioners' sugar

**1.** Heat oven to 350°F.

**2.** In a medium bowl, combine egg yolks and ¼ cup of the granulated sugar. Beat until thick and smooth. Add orange peel and stir to combine. Set aside.

**3.** In another medium bowl, beat egg whites with cream of tartar until thick. Add the remaining ¼ cup granulated sugar and continue to beat until stiff peaks form.

**4.** Add a third of the whites to the yolk mixture and stir to blend. Sift half of the cake flour over the batter. Using a rubber spatula, fold in flour. Add another third of the whites and fold in. Sift remaining cake flour over batter and fold in, then fold in remaining whites.

**5.** Fit a pastry bag with an open round tip and fill with batter. Push batter out onto a greased cookie sheet in a controlled line to form cookies 4 inches long and 1½ inches wide.

Space cookies 2 inches apart. If possible, use a second greased cookie sheet to bake all the cookies at once. (Batter is delicate and deflates quickly.) Sift confectioners' sugar liberally over the cookies through a small fine-meshed sieve.

**6.** Bake until cookies are lightly golden, about 10 minutes. Using a spatula, transfer cookies to a rack and let cool.

*Store cookies in an airtight plastic storage bag at room temperature for up to 3 days. These cookies may be frozen in a tightly covered container for up to 6 months.*

# Orange Marmalade Cookies

As these cookies bake, the orange marmalade oozes out of the dough just enough to caramelize the bottoms and glaze the tops. The crust is cheesy, not sweet, and is the perfect foil for the bittersweet marmalade.

*Makes about 22 cookies*

. . . . . . . . . . . . .

*1 cup (2 sticks) unsalted butter, at room temperature*
*4 ounces cream cheese, at room temperature*
*1 large egg*
*2 cups all-purpose flour*
*1 cup orange marmalade*

**1.** In a mixing bowl, cream together butter and cream cheese until well blended. Add egg and blend until smooth. Stir in flour to form a dough. Wrap dough in plastic wrap and refrigerate at least 3 hours.

**2.** Heat oven to 350°F.

**3.** Divide chilled dough in half. Working with one-half at a time, turn out onto a floured surface and roll into a 12-inch square. Spread surface of each square of dough evenly with ½ cup of the marmalade.

**4.** Roll up each square of dough jelly-roll style. Trim and discard uneven ends. Cut crosswise slices, 1 inch thick, and transfer them to greased cookie sheets, cut side down and 1 inch apart. (Dough will be very soft and will resemble the petals of an opened flower when placed on the cookie sheet.)

**5.** Bake until cookies are browned on the bottom and glazed on top, about 15 minutes. Using a spatula, transfer cookies to a rack and let cool.

*Store cookies in an airtight jar or tin at room temperature for up to 3 days. These cookies may also be frozen in a tightly covered container for up to 6 months.*

This dough may be refrigerated for up to 5 days, or frozen for up to 3 months. Thaw before using.

# Mint-Iced Sugar Cookies

These old-fashioned favorites guarantee a buttery mouthful of home-baked goodness with every bite.

*Makes about 18 cookies*

. . . . . . . . . . . . . . .

*1 cup (2 sticks) unsalted butter,
   at room temperature
½ cup granulated sugar
2 large eggs
1 teaspoon vanilla extract
2 cups all-purpose flour
Mint Cream Icing (recipe follows)*

**1.** Heat oven to 375°F.

**2.** In a mixing bowl, cream butter and sugar until smooth. Add eggs and vanilla and blend. Stir in flour.

**3.** Fit a pastry bag with an open round tip and fill with cookie dough. Push dough out of bag onto greased cookie sheets, shaping it into 3-inch circles, squares, triangles, or zigzags. Space shapes about 1 inch apart.

**4.** Bake just until bottom edges of cookies are beginning to brown, about 10 minutes. Using a spatula, transfer cookies to a rack to cool.

**5.** When cookies have cooled completely, drizzle tops with Mint Cream Icing.

*Store cookies in an airtight plastic storage bag at room temperature for up to 3 days. These cookies may also be frozen in a tightly covered container for up to 6 months.*

This dough may be used immediately or covered with plastic wrap and refrigerated for up to 5 days, or frozen for up to 3 months. Thaw before using.

MINT CREAM ICING
*1 cup confectioners' sugar*
*5-6 tablespoons whipping cream*
*1 teaspoon peppermint extract*

**1.** In a bowl, stir together sugar, cream, and peppermint extract until smoothly blended. Use enough cream to obtain an icing that falls heavily and slowly off a spoon.

**2.** Immediately drizzle icing over tops of cooled cookies. Let icing harden before serving the cookies.

# Soft Molasses Cookies

Deeply flavored and darkly colored with molasses, these cookies are pure Americana. Sorghum syrup can be substituted for the molasses (and was, in years past).

*Makes about 20 cookies*

• • • • • • • • • • • • •

2 cups all-purpose flour
¾ teaspoon cinnamon
½ teaspoon ginger
¼ teaspoon nutmeg
½ teaspoon baking soda
½ teaspoon salt
¼ cup (½ stick) unsalted butter, at room temperature
¼ cup granulated sugar, plus 1 tablespoon for garnish
1 large egg
2 tablespoons rum, light or dark
2 tablespoons milk
½ cup dark molasses

**1.** Combine flour, spices, baking soda, and salt in a bowl. Mix and set aside.

**2.** In a separate bowl, cream butter and ¼ cup sugar until smooth. Add egg, rum, and milk and blend. Add flour mixture, alternating with molasses until dough is formed. Cover bowl with plastic wrap and refrigerate for at least 1 hour.

**3.** Heat oven to 375°F.

**4.** Turn out dough onto a lightly floured surface and roll out to ¼-inch thickness. Using a 2½-inch cookie cutter, cut dough into shapes. Reroll scraps and cut to use all the dough.

**5.** Arrange dough shapes on a greased cookie sheet, spacing them 1 inch apart. Sprinkle tops with the sugar reserved for garnish.

**6.** Bake until cookies are just firm to the touch, about 10 minutes. (Do not overbake.) Using a spatula, transfer cookies to a rack and let cool.

*Store cookies in an airtight plastic storage bag at room temperature for up to 3 days. These cookies may also be frozen in a tightly covered container for up to 6 months.*

This dough may be refrigerated for up to 5 days, or frozen for up to 3 months. Thaw before using.

# Sour Cream Jumbles

Creamy and soft with that sweet, old-fashioned taste, this delightful cookie will appeal to kids of all ages.

*Makes about 26 cookies*

• • • • • • • • • • • • • • •

½ cup (1 stick) unsalted butter, at room temperature
1 cup granulated sugar
½ cup sour cream
1 teaspoon vanilla extract
2 cups all-purpose flour
½ teaspoon baking soda
¼ teaspoon salt
¼ teaspoon nutmeg

**1.** In a mixing bowl, cream together butter and sugar until smooth. Add sour cream and vanilla and blend.

**2.** In a separate bowl, mix together flour, baking soda, and salt and add to creamed mixture. Wrap dough in plastic wrap and refrigerate for at least 1 hour.

**3.** Heat oven to 375°F.

**4.** Divide chilled dough in half and roll out each half between 2 sheets of waxed paper to a thickness of ¼ inch. Peel off top piece of waxed paper and use a 2½-inch cookie cutter to cut dough into shapes. Reroll any dough scraps and cut to use all the dough. Repeat with remaining half of dough.

**5.** Arrange dough shapes on ungreased cookie sheets, spacing them 2 inches apart. Sprinkle tops lightly with nutmeg.

**6.** Bake until bottom edges of cookies have just begun to brown, about 10 minutes. Using a spatula, transfer cookies to a rack and let cool.

*Store cookies in an airtight jar or tin. Baked cookies may be frozen for up to 6 months.*

This dough may be refrigerated for up to 5 days. Do not freeze.

# 3
# Bar Cookies

# Chewy Coconut Bars

The success of these easy-to-make bar cookies lies in the exciting contrast of chewy, sweet coconut harmoniously combined with the slightly tart taste of dried cranberries or cherries. A cookie to remember!

*Makes about 15 bar cookies*

• • • • • • • • • • • • • •

½ *cup all-purpose flour*
1 *teaspoon cinnamon*
¼ *teaspoon baking soda*
¼ *teaspoon salt*
½ *cup (1 stick) unsalted butter,*
   *at room temperature*
½ *cup packed light brown sugar*
1 *large egg*
1½ *cups sweetened shredded*
   *coconut*
½ *cup dried fruit, such as*
   *cranberries or tart cherries*

1. Heat oven to 350°F.

2. Combine flour, cinnamon, baking soda, and salt in a bowl. Mix and set aside.

3. In a separate bowl, cream butter and sugar until smooth. Add egg and blend. Add flour mixture and blend. Stir in coconut and dried fruit until thoroughly mixed.

4. Spread evenly into an ungreased 8-inch square baking pan. Bake until cookies are firm to the touch and browned, about 20 minutes.

5. Place pan on rack and let cool. When cookies are cool, cut into 2½″ × 1½″ bars.

*Store cookies covered in the baking pan at room temperature for up to 3 days, or freeze them in a tightly covered container for up to 6 months.*

# Fig Sandwich Fingers

A sweet, fruity filling is sandwiched between two layers of nutty cookie crust in this treat. A glass of milk is the ideal companion for this cookie.

*Makes about 18 bar cookies*

• • • • • • • • • • • • • • •

1½ cups all-purpose flour
⅔ cup packed light brown sugar
½ cup (1 stick) plus 2 tablespoons unsalted butter, at room temperature
½ cup finely chopped walnuts
1 cup finely chopped dried figs
½ teaspoon dried lemon peel
¼ cup dark corn syrup

**1.** Heat oven to 350°F.

**2.** In a mixing bowl, stir together flour and sugar. Cut in butter until mixture is coarsely crumbled and butter is evenly dispersed. Add walnuts and mix until finely crumbled. Set aside.

**3.** In a separate bowl, combine figs and lemon peel and mix. Add corn syrup and stir until thoroughly combined.

**4.** Spread 1½ cups of the crumb mixture into an ungreased 8-inch square baking pan. Press to pack evenly in pan bottom. Spread fig mixture in an even layer over crumb mixture in pan. Sprinkle remaining crumb mixture over fig layer and press gently to completely enclose the filling.

**5.** Bake until cookies are golden brown, about 25 minutes. Place pan on rack and let cool. When cookies are completely cool, cut into 2½″ × 1¼″ bars.

*Store cookies covered in the baking pan at room temperature for up to 5 days. Do not freeze.*

# Big Fudge Melties

Sweet chocolate chips soften into a velvet topping that prolongs the pleasure of this thick, chewy brownie. It literally melts in your mouth.

*Makes about 9 bar cookies*

· · · · · · · · · · · · · · · ·

4 ounces unsweetened chocolate
½ cup (1 stick) plus 2
    tablespoons unsalted butter
3 large eggs
1¼ cups granulated sugar
1 tablespoon instant coffee
    granules
1½ teaspoons vanilla extract
¾ cup all-purpose flour
1 cup semisweet chocolate chips

1. Heat oven to 350°F.

2. Cut unsweetened chocolate and butter into pieces. Combine in the top of a double boiler and melt over barely simmering water or in a microwave oven for 2½ minutes at High power until melted. Stir until smooth, remove from heat, and set aside to cool.

3. In a mixing bowl, combine eggs, sugar, instant coffee, and vanilla. Beat with an electric mixer on medium speed until mixture is light in color and thick, about 1 minute. Reduce speed to low, add chocolate mixture, and blend. Stir in the flour.

4. Pour batter into a greased 8-inch square baking pan and spread evenly. Bake until center feels firm to the touch, about 25 minutes.

5. Place pan on rack and immediately sprinkle chocolate chips on cookies, spreading with a thin metal spatula until chocolate has melted into a smooth, even layer. Let cool. Cut into 2½-inch squares.

*Store cookies covered in the baking pan at room temperature for up to 3 days. These cookies may also be frozen in a tightly covered container for up to 6 months.*

# Love Those Lemon Dreams

Home bakers have been serving up these delectable bar cookies for decades. Their timeless appeal lies in the contrasts of flavor and texture—a silken, sweet-tart topping over a rich, crumbly crust.

*Makes about 12 bar cookies*

. . . . . . . . . . . . . .

½ cup (1 stick) unsalted butter, at room temperature

⅓ cup confectioners' sugar, plus 1 tablespoon for garnish

1 cup plus 2 tablespoons all-purpose flour

2 large whole eggs and 1 egg yolk

¾ cup granulated sugar

3 tablespoons freshly squeezed lemon juice (about 1 lemon)

**1.** Heat oven to 350°F.

**2.** In a bowl, cream butter and ⅓ cup confectioners' sugar until smooth. Add 1 cup flour and mix to form a crumbly dough.

**3.** Spread into an ungreased 8-inch square baking pan and press to pack evenly in the bottom of the pan. Bake until lightly golden, about 15 minutes.

**4.** Meanwhile, beat eggs and egg yolk in a mixing bowl until foamy. Add granulated sugar and 2 tablespoons flour and beat until thick and smooth. Add lemon juice and blend.

**5.** When crust is baked, remove from oven and pour lemon topping over the hot crust. Return to oven and bake until topping is set and golden brown, about 15 minutes. Place pan on a rack and let cool.

**6.** When cookies are cool, sift 1 tablespoon confectioners' sugar evenly over the top. Cut into 2½″ × 2″ bars.

*Store cookies covered in the baking pan at room temperature for up to 2 days, or in the refrigerator for up to 3 days. Do not freeze.*

# Maple Walnut Tassies

Maple-flavored caramel loaded with walnuts sits atop a divine cream cheese crust in these cookies.

*Makes about 16 bar cookies*

. . . . . . . . . . . . . .

1 cup (2 sticks) unsalted butter, at room temperature
1 3-ounce package cream cheese, at room temperature
¼ cup confectioners' sugar
1 cup all-purpose flour
¼ cup pure maple syrup
⅔ cup packed light brown sugar
¼ cup whipping cream
1½ cups walnut pieces

**1.** Heat oven to 350°F.

**2.** In a mixing bowl, cream ½ cup (1 stick) of butter with cream cheese until smooth. Add confectioners' sugar and blend. Stir in flour and mix to form a crumbly dough.

**3.** Spread dough in an ungreased 8-inch square baking pan and press dough to pack it into the bottom of the pan. Bake until lightly golden, about 15 minutes.

**4.** While crust is baking, combine the remaining ½ cup butter with maple syrup in a saucepan. Cook over medium heat until butter melts, then add brown sugar and stir to dissolve. Bring to a rolling boil and continue to boil for 2 minutes. Remove from heat and stir in cream and walnuts.

**5.** When crust is baked, remove from oven and immediately pour maple topping over the hot crust. Return pan to oven and bake until topping is bubbling but center is firm when pan is shaken, about 25 minutes.

**6.** Place pan on a rack and let cool. When cookies are completely cool, cut into 2-inch squares.

*Store cookies covered in the baking pan at room temperature for up to 5 days. These cookies may also be frozen in a tightly covered container for up to 6 months.*

# Sweet Persimmon Fireside Cookies

108

These bar cookies are a delightful way to enjoy the exotic flavor of the crimson-toned persimmon.

*Makes about 16 bar cookies*

. . . . . . . . . . . . . .

2 cups all-purpose flour
½ cup cake flour
1 teaspoon cinnamon
1 teaspoon ginger
½ teaspoon baking soda
¼ teaspoon salt
½ cup (1 stick) unsalted butter,
   at room temperature
1 cup granulated sugar
Grated rind of 1 lemon
1 cup pureed ripe persimmon
   pulp (about 2 medium
   persimmons)
1 large egg
¼ cup confectioners' sugar

1. Heat oven to 375°F.

2. Combine both flours, cinnamon, ginger, baking soda, and salt in a bowl. Mix and set aside.

3. In a separate bowl, cream butter, granulated sugar, and lemon rind until fluffy and smooth. Add persimmon pulp and egg and blend. Gradually add flour mixture and mix until blended.

4. Pour batter into a greased 9″ × 13″ baking pan and spread out evenly. Bake until cookies are golden brown and a cake tester inserted in the center comes out clean, about 25 minutes.

5. Place pan on rack and let cool. When cookies are completely cool, sift confectioners' sugar evenly over the top. Cut into 3″ × 2″ bars.

*Store cookies covered in the baking pan at room temperature for up to 3 days. These cookies may also be frozen in a tightly covered container for up to 6 months.*

# Rocky Road Cookies

Here's a scrumptious brownie-style bar cookie, loaded with milk chocolate, streaks of melting marshmallows, and crunchy walnuts.

*Makes about 12 bar cookies*

. . . . . . . . . . . . . .

6 ounces milk chocolate
¼ cup (½ stick) unsalted butter
2 large eggs
1 cup all-purpose flour
¼ teaspoon baking soda
¼ teaspoon salt
1 cup milk chocolate chips
1 cup miniature marshmallows
1 cup coarsely chopped walnuts

1. Heat oven to 325°F.

2. Cut chocolate into pieces. Place chocolate and butter in the top of a double boiler or in a microwavable dish. Melt over barely simmering water in the double boiler or for 2½ minutes at High power in a microwave oven. Remove from heat, stir smooth, and set aside.

3. In a mixing bowl, beat eggs until foamy. Add melted chocolate mixture and blend smooth.

4. In a separate bowl, mix together flour, baking soda, and salt. Add to chocolate mixture and blend. Stir in chocolate chips, marshmallows, and walnuts. (Batter will be thick and stiff.)

5. Pour into a greased 9-inch square baking pan and spread evenly. Bake until cookies are browned and firm to the touch, about 25 minutes.

6. Place pan on a rack and let cool. When cookies are cool, cut into 2½″ × 2″ bars.

*Store cookies covered in the baking pan at room temperature for up to 3 days. These cookies may also be frozen in a tightly covered container for up to 6 months.*

# Index

114

115

116